A Note to Parents

DK READERS is a compelling program for beginning readers, designed in conjunction with leading literacy experts, including Dr. Linda Gambrell, Professor of Education at Clemson University. Dr. Gambrell has served as President of the National Reading Conference, the College Reading Association, and the International Reading Association.

Beautiful illustrations and superb full-color photographs combine with engaging, easy-to-read stories to offer a fresh approach to each subject in the series. Each DK READER is guaranteed to capture a child's interest while developing his or her reading skills, general knowledge, and love of reading.

The five levels of DK READERS are aimed at different reading abilities, enabling you to choose the books that are exactly right for your child:

Pre-level 1: Learning to read
Level 1: Beginning to read
Level 2: Beginning to read alone
Level 3: Reading alone
Level 4: Proficient readers

The "normal" age at which a child begins to read can be anywhere from three to eight years old. Adult participation through the lower levels is very helpful for providing encouragement, discussing storylines, and sounding out unfamiliar words.

No matter which level you select, you can be sure that you are helping your child learn to read, then read to learn!

LONDON, NEW YORK, MUNICH,
MELBOURNE, AND DELHI

For DK/Brady Games
Publisher David Waybright
Editor-in-chief H. Leigh Davis
Licensing Director Mike Degler
International Translations Brian Saliba
Director of Business Development
Michael Vaccaro
Title Manager Tim Fitzpatrick

Reading Consultant
Linda B. Gambrell, Ph.D.

Produced by
Shoreline Publishing Group LLC
President James Buckley Jr.
Designer Tom Carling, carlingdesign.com

For WWE
Director, Home Entertainment & Books
Dean Miller
Photo Department
Frank Vitucci, Joshua Tottenham, Jamie Nelsen
Copy Editor Kevin Caldwell
Legal Lauren Dienes-Middlen

First American Edition, 2009
07 08 09 10 11 10 9 8 7 6 5 4 3 2 1
Published in the United States by DK Publishing
375 Hudson Street, New York, New York 10014

DK books are available at special discounts when purchased in bulk
for sales promotions, premiums, fund-raising, or educational use.
For details, contact: DK Publishing Special Markets,
375 Hudson Street, New York, New York 10014
SpecialSales@dk.com

A catalog record for this book is available
from the Library of Congress.

ISBN: 978-0-7566-5384-2 (Paperback)
ISBN: 978-0-7566-5383-5 (Hardcover)

Printed and bound by Lake Book

The publisher would like to thank the following for their kind
permission to reproduce their photographs:
All photos courtesy WWE Entertainment, Inc.
All other images © Dorling Kindersley
For further information see: www.dkimages.com

Discover more at
www.dk.com

Contents

DK READERS

READING
3
ALONE

Triple H®

Written by Brian Shields

DK Publishing

A sudden start

It was *Monday Night Raw*, October 21, 1996. The fans were pumped up. They had filled the arena and were waiting for great WWE action. They were supposed to witness a match pitting the popular Mr. Perfect against a lesser-known Superstar with the odd name of Hunter Hearst-Helmsley.

Helmsley waited in the ring for his opponent. Mr. Perfect strode into the ring to thunderous applause. Standing beside him was "Wildman" Marc Mero, the reigning WWE Intercontinental Champion.

Hearst-Helmsley faces off against Mr. Perfect (right).

Helmsley and Mr. Perfect glared at each other. The fight was moments from getting started and the fans were ready!

Suddenly, WWE officials stepped in and broke the spell. They told Mr. Perfect that he couldn't compete that night due to an injury. The crowd was stunned. What came next was even more startling.

Helmsley stuns the crowd by defeating Marc Mero!

Mr. Perfect told the officials and Helmsley that Marc Mero would compete in his place. That's when things got really interesting.

Young Helmsley hesitated at first, and then challenged Mero. "If the WWE Intercontinental Championship is on the line, I'll fight him," he said.

"Then let's get it on!" Mero shouted. Helmsley would compete that night after all, but for a championship!

Helmsley pinned Mero, taking the match and winning his first championship in WWE. Hunter Hearst-Helmsley was now at the top of the WWE world. But the  skinny kid from New England—you know him today as Triple H—sure didn't start out that way.

Weightlifting is still a big part of Triple H's daily routine.

The early years

Triple H was born in Nashua, New Hampshire.

To look at him now, you might think that he was a big, strong, tough kid when he was growing up. But nothing could be further from the truth.

Triple H called himself a 135-pound (61 kg) "gangly beanpole," tall and skinny. That didn't stop him from being a huge WWE fan. His favorite Superstar when he was a kid was Ric Flair.

Then came the event that changed the future Superstar's life. When he was 14 years old, Triple H got a free one-week membership to a small, local gym. He fell in love with bodybuilding and began a regular schedule of working out.

During the next three years, Triple H was in the gym every day. The scrawny kid changed into a 6'4" (1.9 m), 210-pound (95-kg) powerhouse. He began entering—and winning—bodybuilding events throughout New Hampshire.

At the age of 19, he won the Teenage Mr. New Hampshire title. But bodybuilding was just a stepping stone.

"I never seriously considered becoming a pro bodybuilder," he later said. "My dream was World Wrestling Entertainment!"

"Killer" Kowalski

Legendary champion Walter "Killer" Kowalski competed professionally for thirty years from 1947–1977, winning many heavyweight and tag-team championships. When he retired from the ring, Kowalski started the Pro Wrestling School, training future stars like Triple H.

The mighty Triple H is not a "scrawny kid" anymore!

The teenager knew that to realize that dream he would need training. He enrolled in a school run by WWE Hall-of-Famer Walter "Killer" Kowalski.

A Superstar at last

In May 1995, Triple H joined WWE, competing under the name Hunter Hearst-Helmsley, the "Connecticut Blueblood." ("Blueblood" means a person born into a very high-class, usually rich family.) Making his debut on April 30, 1995, he defeated opponents with his classic finishing move, the "Pedigree." Playing off his "Blueblood" nickname, he made videos about good manners.

After dropping that nickname, the Superstar still known as Hunter Hearst-Helmsley quickly became buddies with a group of top WWE Superstars. Along with the "Heartbreak Kid" Shawn Michaels, Kevin Nash (competing under the name "Diesel"), "1-2-3 Kid", and

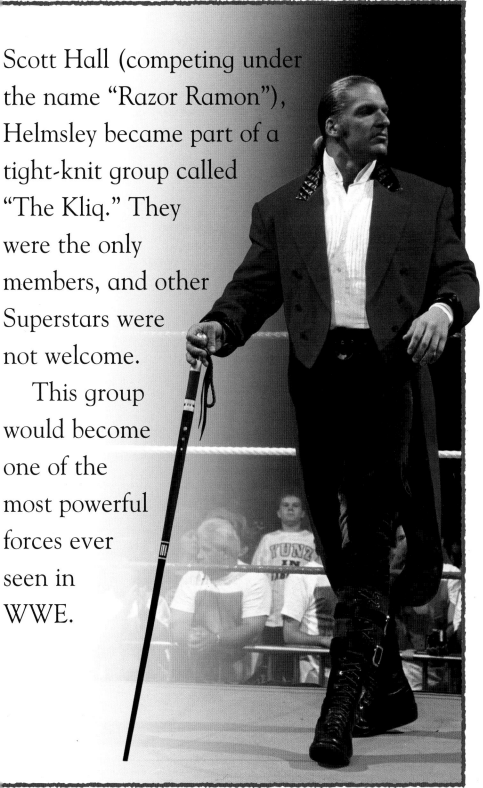

Scott Hall (competing under the name "Razor Ramon"), Helmsley became part of a tight-knit group called "The Kliq." They were the only members, and other Superstars were not welcome.

This group would become one of the most powerful forces ever seen in WWE.

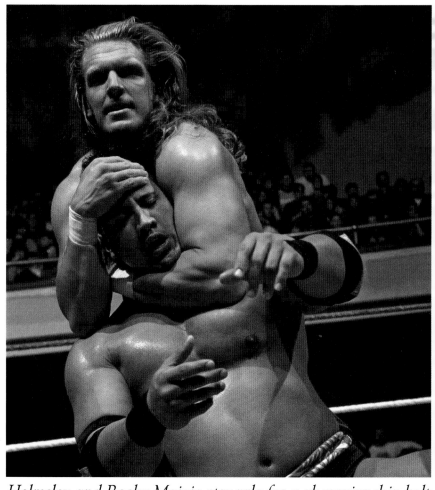

Helmsley and Rocky Maivia struggle for a championship belt.

The Kliq grew to great power in WWE.
Helmsley earned a place in *WrestleMania
XII*. Under the spotlight of WWE's
biggest event, he tasted disappointment,
losing to Ultimate Warrior.

But Helmsley got his chance to make up for the defeat on *Monday Night Raw* in October 1996. In that surprise, unscheduled match in which he was supposed to battle Mr. Perfect, he ended up beating "Wildman" Marc Mero to win the WWE Intercontinental Championship.

He held it for four months before losing it to Rocky Maivia in 1997. Maivia would go on to become the WWE Superstar (and later, international movie star) known as The Rock.

Triple H's WWE Championship History
- WWE Heavyweight Champion
- World Heavyweight Champion
- Intercontinental Champion
- European Championship
- World Tag Team Champion

King of the Ring

Following the loss of his title, Helmsley worked even harder to get back to the top. In 1997, he entered the *King of the Ring* tournament, a single-elimination event. The rules said that if you lost one match, you had to go

Helmsley became the King of the Ring in 1997.

Tag Team

A tag team is a pair of Superstars. They compete one at a time against an opposing tag team. Usually, one member from each tag team is in the ring at a time. In order to leave the ring and exchange places with his teammate, a Superstar must tag his teammate, who can then take his place in the ring.

home. To continue competing, a Superstar had to keep winning. That's exactly what he did, over and over!

In the quarterfinals, he took on and defeated Crush, a WWE World Tag Team Champion. Next up for Helmsley in the semifinals was Ahmed Johnson, a former WWE Intercontinental Champion. Executing a perfect Pedigree, Helmsley won again, advancing to the finals.

In the *King of the Ring* Finals, Helmsley faced off against Mankind, former holder of a World Tag Team Championship, the first WWE Hardcore Championship, and the WWE Championship. In the longest match of the event—just under twenty minutes—Helmsley beat Mankind to win the tournament.

Mankind was no match for Triple H, the new "King."

The young man who started out lifting weights in New Hampshire had seen his dream come true. He had become the *King of the Ring.*

Around this time, Helmsley joined a new group of WWE Superstars. They called themselves "D-Generation X," or DX for short. Helmsley teamed up with his Kliq buddy the "Heartbreak Kid" Shawn Michaels, "Ravishing" Rick Rude, and Chyna, who also served as his bodyguard. When he joined DX, he also shortened his name to Triple H.

TRIPLE H

Led by Michaels, DX quickly became the rebels of WWE. They broke rules, made fun of other WWE Superstars, and pretty much said and did whatever they wanted.

This wild and brash behavior confused fans, because two of the DX rebels were also WWE titleholders. Shawn Michaels was the WWE Champion, and Triple H was the WWE European Champion during the time they were both members of DX.

At *WrestleMania XIV* in Boston, both Shawn Michaels and Triple H competed in featured matches, putting their championships on the line. It would be a memorable evening in the ring.

The two DX teammates got together that night—but not by choice! During Michaels' match against "Stone Cold" Steve Austin, Michaels flipped over the top rope, tumbled out of the ring, and landed right on top of Triple H!

Triple H was part of the mighty DX.

To get back at Austin and help his friend and DX partner, Triple H tossed Austin through the crowd barrier around the ring. However, once both Superstars were back in the ring, Austin defeated Michaels to take away his WWE Championship.

At the same event, Triple H faced off against longtime rival

Triple H successfully defends his title!

Owen Hart to defend his WWE European Championship.

Hart had the upper hand early on, unleashing a powerbomb and a sharpshooter. In the end, Triple H used his Pedigree move to win the match and keep his title.

Then, in a move that stunned the sports entertainment world, Shawn Michaels announced that he was leaving WWE. With Michaels' departure, Triple H became the new leader of DX and announced that his old buddy from the Kliq, the 1-2-3 Kid, was joining the group under the new name X-Pac. Joining them were Chyna, "Road Dogg" Jesse James, and Billy Gunn.

Triple H used all the tools he had to defeat The Rock.

"The Game"

DX's position as the top group in WWE was soon challenged by the Nation of Domination. This group was led by a rising WWE Superstar, The Rock. A rivalry quickly developed between the two leaders, The Rock and Triple H.

This heated rivalry came to a head at *SummerSlam '98*, where the two battled for the WWE Intercontinental Championship in a Ladder Match. Triple H opened by hitting The Rock with a clothesline that dropped him to the mat. Triple H tried a Pedigree, but The Rock reversed it and threw him over the top rope. The Rock started up the ladder, but Triple H knocked him off and went up in his place. Snatching the belt, he became a champion again!

Ladder Match
In a Ladder Match, a championship belt is hung high above the ring. A ladder is placed in the ring, and the first competitor to climb the ladder and grab the belt is the winner.

Triple H now had another championship and was the leader of DX. He was on a roll when he entered *WrestleMania XV* in March 1999. There he beat Kane.

Triple H hoists the WWE Championship!

But Triple H had another surprise to add to his record of stunning moves: He announced that he was leaving DX. The other members of the group were shocked.

Later that summer, though he had already earned many great titles, Triple H finally got a chance at the biggest prize of all: the WWE Championship.

On August 23, 1999, during *Monday Night Raw*, Triple H beat Mankind to capture his first WWE Championship. Triple H left no doubt that night. He was now the greatest Superstar in the world. With this title came the nickname that would define the rest of his career. Triple H became known as "The Game."

Triple H shows The Rock who is the boss!

Riding high as WWE Champion, Triple H married Stephanie McMahon, daughter of Mr. McMahon, the Chairman of WWE.

In an odd twist of fate, Triple H lost his title to Mr. McMahon himself in September's *SmackDown*.

But the force of nature that is Triple H was not to be denied. At *Unforgiven*, Triple H regained his WWE Championship title in a Six-Pack Challenge. To reclaim the belt, he had to beat The Rock, Mankind, Kane, Big Show, and Davey Boy Smith, the British Bulldog. Taking on and defeating five other opponents, Triple H showed once again why he was The Game.

Six-Pack Challenge

A Six-Pack Challenge is a match in which six Superstars compete. Two are in the ring battling while the other four wait outside the ropes. Whenever one competitor leaves the ring, another can take his place. This free-for-all is one of the most exciting matches in sports entertainment.

At *WrestleMania 2000*, Triple H once again put his championship on the line. This time it was against the

A determined Triple H prepares to defend the WWE Championship.

dangerous trio of Big Show, The Rock, and Triple H's arch rival, Mick Foley, in a Four Corners Match.

Yet, the powerful Triple H took on all three of those top-tanked opponents at the same time. At the end of the match, Triple H was the last man standing.

Next up for "The Game" was a surprising team-up with his former enemy, Stone Cold Steve Austin, in 2001. At the time, Triple H was the WWE Intercontinental Champion and Austin was the overall WWE Champion. Together, these two talented Superstars competed in tag team matches, calling themselves "The Two-Man Power Trip." It would be prove to be one of the greatest teams ever.

Both Triple H and Stone Cold looked to add another title to their collection. At *Backlash 2001*, the "Two-Man Power Trip" took on Kane & Undertaker, together known as the "Brothers of Destruction." This match was for the WWE World Tag Team Championship.

Austin (left) and Triple H were an unstoppable force.

Competing like the champions they already were, the "Two-Man Power Trip" defeated the "Brothers of Destruction" to become World Tag Team Champions.

Now referred to as the "Golden Team," the duo held all three of the top WWE titles. This was only the second time in WWE history that a tag team held all three top titles.

It looked like everything was working out for Triple H as he continued to make his dreams come true. But as he stood at the peak of the WWE world, disaster was lurking around the corner.

Injury and return

In May 2001, one month
after capturing the World
Tag Team titles, the "Two-
Man Power Trip" defended
their belt against a team led
by Chris Jericho. When
Jericho had Stone Cold
trapped in his Walls of Jericho
hold, Triple H ran over to
help. As he did, he tore a
muscle in his left leg.

His injury was so serious
that Triple H had to be carried from the
ring. The tear in his muscle required an
operation, which kept him out of action
for eight long months. The doctors told
him that his WWE career was over. The
physical therapy and rehabilitation

WWE officials assist the injured Superstar.

process was just too much for an
ordinary man to bring himself back into
the shape a WWE Superstar needed to
compete against the world's best. But
"The Game" was no ordinary man.

Triple H worked hard for eight months, doing his rehab exercises, practicing his moves, and training to the max. He was out to prove the doctors wrong, and that was exactly what he did.

On January 7, 2002, eight months after his injury, Triple H made his return to the ring on *Monday Night Raw*. That was just a warm-up. At *WrestleMania X-8*, he took on Chris Jericho for the Undisputed WWE Championship. The winner would be the king of WWE.

Despite Jericho's repeated attacks on Triple H's surgically repaired leg, Triple H stood his ground and beat Jericho with a Pedigree. The victory completed his amazing return from injury. Triple H had come all the way back to the top!

The walls of Jericho tumbled to Triple H's power.

Evolution

Triple H's former DX buddy Shawn
Michaels shocked fans when he returned
to WWE in 2002. Fans assumed that
Michaels would rejoin Triple H and
reform DX. But during a DX event,
Triple H turned against his former
teammate. The two immediately became
bitter rivals.

Their rivalry came to head at
SummerSlam 2002. There, Triple H
battled Michaels in a Street Fight. This
all-out brawl was a grudge match, plain

Street Fight

A Street Fight is a match in which WWE's
normal rules and holds are thrown out the
window. Anything goes. Any object can be used,
and a competitor can pin his opponent to win the
match anywhere, not just inside the ring.

Michaels stunned WWE fans by beating "The Game."

and simple. Michaels was after Triple H
for turning his back on him, and The
Game was out to prove that the days of
DX were gone forever. In the end,
Michaels beat Triple H.

"Evolution": Batista, Triple H, Ric Flair, and Randy Orto

In January 2003, Triple H started his own group. He teamed up with his childhood hero, "Nature Boy" Ric Flair, and young Superstars Batista and Randy

Orton. He called his new team "Evolution."

The men who were part of the Evolution team wore fancy suits, drove expensive cars, and flew in their own private airplane. They also held the three top titles in WWE. Triple H was the World Heavyweight Champion, Randy Orton was the Intercontinental Champion, and Batista and Ric Flair were the World Tag Team Champions.

Evolution was beating all of WWE's best. During his time as the leader of the group, Triple H successfully defended his championship against Goldberg, Rob Van Dam, "Big Poppa Pump" Scott Steiner, Shawn Michaels, Kevin Nash, and Booker T—a who's who of WWE Superstars.

At *WrestleMania XX* in March 2004, Triple H finally lost his World Heavyweight Championship. Then, as always happens, even with the most talented teams, Evolution broke up in 2005. The four Superstars went their own ways.

The following year, the always-unpredictable Triple H pulled another shocker when he joined with former rival Shawn Michaels to reform DX. This D-Generation X revival tore through WWE, beating The Spirit Squad, Umaga and Big Show, and the most powerful family in WWE, the McMahons.

The year 2007 started off badly. In January, during a match between DX and Rated-RKO (Edge & Randy Orton), Triple H injured his right leg.

*Triple H battles Edge
for the title in 2007.*

Again, he had surgery and was sidelined
for months.

A 2007 championship made Triple H the "King of Kings.

"King of Kings"

Triple H made his return to the ring at *SummerSlam 2007*, where he battled and defeated King Booker. After that victory over "The King," Triple H declared himself the *real* king of WWE and picked up a new nickname, the "King of Kings."

A return to the championship ranks came later in 2007 at *No Mercy*. There, Triple H battled Randy Orton, and beat him to recapture the WWE Championship for the eleventh time in his long and amazing career.

Throughout a busy and successful 2008, Triple H defended his title against Edge, The Great Khali, and Jeff Hardy. He finally lost the championship to Edge in November of that year, at the *2008 Survivor Series*.

The "King of Kings" remains a fixture in the exciting world of WWE. Triple H has won every championship and honor there is in sports-entertainment. A spot in the WWE Hall of Fame is all but guaranteed for him someday.

But the man they call "The Game" has taken his talents to other arenas. He has acted in movies such as *Blade: Trinity*. And he has appeared on TV, in shows such as *Pacific Blue*, *The Drew Carey Show*, *The Bernie Mac Show*, *MADtv*, and *Saturday Night Live*, and he has made numerous commercials.

Through it all, though, he has kept up a strict routine in the gym, his first love, to stay in shape for that moment when the bell sounds and Triple H springs into the ring.

Glossary

Coveted
Desired, hoped for

Evolution
A gradual process in which something changes into a different form

Feud
An ongoing argument or disagreement

Finishing move
The move a Superstar uses to defeat his or her opponent

Gangly
Tall and slim, though a bit clumsy

Grudge
Longtime bitterness against somebody or something

Hold
In WWE, the way in which a competitor grabs and gets control of his opponent

Lurking
Waiting or creeping

Opponent
Rival, foe, enemy, the person a Superstar fights

Pedigree
The name of Triple H's most famous move, the word also means the family background of a person, usually used to refer to old, high-class families

Physical therapy
Exercises that are done to help rebuild strength in muscles after surgery or an accident

Pin
In WWE, to hold an opponent's shoulders on the mat for a count of three

Rehabilitation
Healing treatment

Ring
Square mat surrounded by ropes in which a WWE match takes place

Scrawny
Skinny

Sidelined
Unable to take part in an activity or event

Surgically repaired
Fixed by undergoing surgery, a difficult medical procedure that usually involves cutting, in a hospital

Thunderous
Loud

Tournament
A competition made up of many individual matches

Undisputed
Unchallenged, with no doubt